Spelling Four

An Interactive Vocabulary & Spelling Workbook for 8-Year-Olds.

(With AudioBook Lessons)

By
Bukky Ekine-Ogunlana

www.tcecpublishing.com

© Copyright Bukky Ekine-Ogunlana 2024 - All rights reserved.

The content of this book may not be reproduced, duplicated, or transmitted without direct written permission from the author or the publisher. Under no circumstance will any blame or legal responsibility be held against the publisher, or author, for any damages, reparation, or monetary loss due to the information contained within this book. Either directly or indirectly. You are responsible for your own choices, actions, and results.

Legal Notice:

This book is copyright protected. This book is only for personal use. You cannot amend, distribute, sell, use, quote, or paraphrase any part, or the content within this book, without the consent of the author or publisher.

Disclaimer Notice:

Please note the information contained within this document is for educational and entertainment purposes only. All effort has been executed to present accurate, up-to-date, reliable, and complete information. No warranties of any kind are declared or implied. Readers acknowledge that the author is not engaging in the rendering of legal, financial, medical, or professional advice. The content within this book has been derived from various sources. Please consult a licensed professional before attempting any techniques outlined in this book.

By reading this document, the reader agrees that under no circumstances is the author responsible for any direct or indirect losses incurred as a result of the use of the information contained within this document, including, but not limited to, errors, omissions, or inaccuracies.

Published by
TCEC Publishing

Table of Contents

Dedication 6
Introduction 7

Spelling 4 - 1 8
Spelling 4 - 2 12
Spelling 4 - 3 16
Spelling 4 - 4 20
Spelling 4 - 5 24
Spelling 4 - 6 28
Spelling 4 - 7 32
Spelling 4 - 8 36
Spelling 4 - 9 40
Spelling 4 - 10 44
Spelling 4 - 11 48
Spelling 4 - 12 52
Spelling 4 - 13 56
Spelling 4 - 14 60
Spelling 4 - 15 64
Spelling 4 - 16 68
Spelling 4 - 17 72
Spelling 4 - 18 76
Spelling 4 - 19 80
Spelling 4 - 20 84

Table of Contents

Spelling 4 - 21 88
Spelling 4 - 22 92
Spelling 4 - 23 96
Spelling 4 - 24 100
Spelling 4 - 25 104

Conclusion 108
Answers 131
Other Books You'll Love! 146
Audiobooks 150
Facebook Community 151
References 153

Dedication

This book is dedicated to our three exceptional children and all the beautiful children worldwide who have passed through the T.C.E.C 6-16 years programme over the years. Thank you for the opportunity to serve you and invest in your colourful and bright future.

Introduction

Welcome to Spelling 4, the fourth Spelling for Kids series book. It is ideal for eight-year-olds. We are happy to see you here!

In Spelling four, 300 new words are waiting for you to conquer them. There is no need to rush or worry. Steady and slow wins the race. It all comes down to the same technique I'm sure you know very well by now.

You can bring a friend to study together if you want, and maybe even make it a contest to see who is doing the best. A little competition never harmed anyone. On the contrary, it can create a challenge and make studying more exciting and fun.

So, get ready because the spelling joyride begins on the next page!

spelling 4-1

1. Spell:

The cool _____ air made George relax.

2. Spell:

He was able to lift the _____ bag of potatoes by himself.

3. Spell:

Having pancakes is my favorite _____.

Spelling 4-1

4. Spell:

I can draw _____ lines without using a ruler.

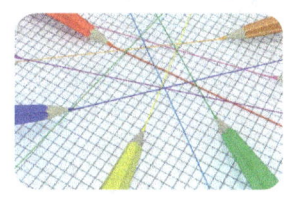

5. Spell:

Kelly had a stiff _____ when he woke from sleep.

6. Spell:

James took the computer devices _____ and fixed them back.

Spelling 4-1

7. Spell:

Working out helps me keep my body in

_____.

8. Spell:

I love these _____ of sneakers!

9. Spell:

The carpenter did _____ a handle to the bathroom door.

Spelling 4-1

10. Spell:

The market square came _____ today because of the musical band.

11. Spell:

The wind blew with so much _____ that it threw away the chairs from the garden.

12. Spell:

It is against the _____ to steal.

Congrats! You have finished learning the words in lesson 1. Remember to know and understand the meaning of all the new words you have found.

Spelling 4-2

1. Spell:

This _____ is so beautiful, full of red and yellow tulips.

2. Spell:

I have everything already packed for my _____, and I can't wait to leave home!

3. Spell:

Christmas is my favorite _____ because I get presents from my family.

Spelling 4-2

4. Spell:

Mangoes grow best in tropical

_____.

5. Spell:

We had a chicken and tomato

_____ for

breakfast.

6. Spell:

_____ presentation, Tom! You

did good work, and I am proud of you!

Spelling 4-2

7. Spell:

The competition was really _____ .

8. Spell:

We did not _____ the test on time because there were insufficient pencils.

9. Spell:

When Adam is sad, he becomes _____ and does not want to hang out with us.

Spelling 4-2

10. Spell:

I _____ it was Ella who cleared up the kitchen.

11. Spell:

There was only one _____ in his taxi.

12. Spell:

Lilian must _____ her brother to the library to complete his research.

You've made it! You completed lesson 2. Pay attention, kids; if you find it difficult to learn some words, you should write them down on paper. That will help you remember them better.

Spelling 4-3

1. Spell:

Danny is now reading the last

_____ of his book.

2. Spell:

_____ A808 from New York to Disneyland was canceled due to extreme weather conditions.

3. Spell:

This _____ was withdrawn from the market because it was found dangerous to health.

Spelling 4-3

4. Spell:

She has _____ an apology letter for being rude in class.

5. Spell:

He _____ his shirt by accident.

6. Spell:

You have to water the _____ often for the flowers to grow.

Spelling 4-3

7. Spell:

The _____ from the cliff is spectacular!

8. Spell:

She gave _____ yesterday to a set of beautiful twins.

9. Spell:

Writing _____ brings out the most sensitive and creative side of me.

Spelling 4-3

10. Spell:

Jane did _____ cream gently.

11. Spell:

It is _____ sad that you have to go now and leave me.

12. Spell:

This toy's _____ is very high, and I must save a month to buy it.

Well done! You have finished lesson 3. You should be proud of yourself!

spelling 4-4

1. Spell:

She did _____ herself well during the auditioning.

2. Spell:

You _____ me when you burst like that in the room. Can you please knock on the door next time?

3. Spell:

Lois _____ to go with the teenagers because she was unsure what they were up to.

Spelling 4-4

4. Spell:

The trainers are too _____ for Kathy.

5. Spell:

Santa Claus enters the house by the _____ and leaves his presents under the Christmas tree.

6. Spell:

Why did you _____ the water into the mug?

Spelling 4-4

7. Spell:
We do _____ tasks every Friday at school before break time.

8. Spell:
Lilian is going on the speaking _____ to help her improve her speaking skills.

9. Spell:
David's mum was shouting, and you could hear the _____ in her voice.

spelling 4-4

10. Spell:

Mark trained his dog always to

_____ him.

11. Spell:

I always leave a _____ to the homeless man who sleeps outside the church.

12. Spell:

I have an _____! Why don't we throw a surprise get-together for Tom, now that he got out of the hospital?

Congrats! You have finished learning the words in lesson 4.

Spelling 4-5

1. Spell:

Julius went with his dad to spend his Father's Day with his _____.

2. Spell:

Daniel and Helen saw a _____ they had not seen in years at the wedding.

3. Spell:

It has been my _____ to be of service to you.

Spelling 4-5

4. Spell:
Ali flashed the _____ as a signal to his team.

5. Spell:
Who wants _____ cookies with his milk? Mommy asked.

6. Spell:
We should never cross the _____ when the traffic light is red.

Spelling 4-5

7. Spell:

Dad always gets up before _____ every day to have time to work out before going to the office.

8. Spell:

Deric will start work after his exams and get the minimum _____ .

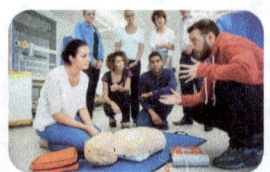

9. Spell:

The class is having a film show on the last day of the school_____.

Spelling 4-5

10. Spell:

Billy left the team because he could not get along with his _____ team members.

11. Spell:

I will _____ your salary if you refuse to accept the other company's offer.

12. Spell:

Noah's train did not _____ from the station on time.

Well done! You have finished lesson 5. You should be proud of yourself!

Spelling 4-6

1. Spell:

Today's lesson was a little _____ and tiresome because there was no interaction with the teacher.

2. Spell:

Trees do turn brown in _____, making them colorful.

3. Spell:

Jude is pleased and satisfied with his _____ income.

Spelling 4-6

4. Spell:

I hid the _____ in my drawer because I wanted to give him the present the next day.

5. Spell:

The school will _____ more teachers to work with the younger children.

6. Spell:

Mike's dog always does _____ him and follows his orders.

Spelling 4-6

7. Spell:

The _____ forecast comes after the evening news.

8. Spell:

We treat you and your sister on _____ terms.

9. Spell:

Lilian heard the sad news of the _____ of her cat.

Spelling 4-6

10. Spell:

My parents thinks that they will

_____ me if they do me all

the favors.

11. Spell:

There was a massive _____

of people in front of the

game shop.

12. Spell:

Well, that had been a pretty

_____ exam, but

I managed to score high

eventually!

You've made it! You completed lesson 6.

Spelling 4-7

1. Spell:
Noah's dad did _____ him to do his house chore before playing football.

2. Spell:
It did _____ to me to take my umbrella along.

3. Spell:
Abraham did not add _____ to his food because his mummy was not around.

Spelling 4-7

4. Spell:

The new toy did not _____ the little girl because she preferred the old one.

5. Spell:

King Kong was the name of a _____ gorilla featured in an old yet popular American movie.

6. Spell:

The trainee nurse could not locate the blood _____ , so the midwife had to do it.

Spelling 4-7

7. Spell:

The mosquito is a very annoying

_____ .

8. Spell:

Why don't you use a clean _____ for your face? I have many in the bathroom drawer.

9. Spell:

As much as you seem to _____ your homework, you really have no choice but to do it.

Spelling 4-7

10. Spell:

Dad always reads the _____ while drinking his coffee in the morning.

11. Spell:

Riding the _____ to school and back makes my day!

12. Spell:

Jeremiah wanted to play volleyball tonight; _____ , his headache kept him aside.

Great! Lesson 7 is over!

Spelling 4-8

1. Spell:

There was an _____ smell coming from his room.

2. Spell:

The _____ is a number, word, or letter before another word.

3. Spell:

The dance competition was a huge _____ .

spelling 4-8

4. Spell:

I prefer talking to him in

_____ and not by phone.

5. Spell:

_____ your best, Mike! I

believe in you!

6. Spell:

It will not be _____ for me

to change school in January.

Spelling 4-8

7. Spell:

He did _____ a few people for the final rehearsal.

8. Spell:

Your _____ matters!

9. Spell:

Liam is the most _____ boy in the class; he finds it challenging to stay calm.

Spelling 4-8

10. Spell:

His uncle was _____ for coming to pick him up late for the match.

11. Spell:

My sister gave a _____ reminder to my dad so he could remember her birthday gift.

12. Spell:

The woman had a conversation with her _____ about coming later.

Well done! You have finished lesson 8. You should be proud of yourself!

Spelling 4-9

1. Spell:

My favorite thing is drinking _____ with my buddy in the café down the street.

2. Spell:

Cool! The _____ of that pool is very long; you should enjoy swimming in it!

3. Spell:

Distractions are the worst _____ of your concentration when you study.

Spelling 4-9

4. Spell:

She did not _____ to the email on time.

5. Spell:

My _____ aches when I see a lost and injured dog on the street.

6. Spell:

There will be a new school _____ in September for the older kids.

Spelling 4-9

7. Spell:

We did not _____ the answers and we all got the question right.

8. Spell:

To draw a perfect _____ , you must use a compass.

9. Spell:

I am an American _____ , and I am living in California.

Spelling 4-9

10. Spell:

Listening to that _____ of music makes me relax.

11. Spell:

Julia bought a _____ bag for herself.

12. Spell:

Nina watches and helps her mummy in the _____ .

Fantastic! You have finished the words in lesson 9.

Spelling 4-10

1. Spell:

There is not enough water in the new

_____ .

2. Spell:

You are under oath, so you must be

_____ with the

judge.

3. Spell:

My favorite band is on_____

this summer, and I will get to see them

when they visit my city!

spelling 4-10

4. Spell:

_____ up, Tom! The school bus is already here!

5. Spell:

Slow and _____ wins the race, said the turtle to the hare.

6. Spell:

I know my house _____ .

Spelling 4-10

7. Spell:

I am not allowed to have a Facebook _____ yet.

8. Spell:

David does not know the _____ of things because he is a one-year-old.

9. Spell:

Matt bought all the things for the family _____ on Saturday.

Spelling 4-10

10. Spell:

We had to _____ to London to see our grandma for Mother's Day.

11. Spell:

My favorite _____ is purple.

12. Spell:

Come and _____ us, Mark; we can all play together!

Lesson 10 has come to an end. Awesome!

Spelling 4-11

1. Spell:

The _____ kettle is not working.

2. Spell:

The driver did not _____ the parcel to the address.

3. Spell:

The pilot was able to _____ the plane during the storm.

Spelling 4-11

4. Spell:

Our home is our _____ .

5. Spell:

Visiting Disneyland is my dream

_____ .

6. Spell:

The year four class did a _____ of their drawings.

Spelling 4-11

7. Spell:

Always remember that nothing can come

_____ your

parents and you.

8. Spell:

She _____ a decent letter of

apology.

9. Spell:

Debby lives in a nearby _____.

Spelling 4-11

10. Spell:

Ephraim was full of _____ .

11. Spell:

Our visit to the new _____ room in the neighbourhood was a thrilling experience!

12. Spell:

David did a great _____ for his best friend.

Spelling 4-12

1. Spell:

Twenty minutes _____ to be enough for you to finish your daily spelling practice.

2. Spell:

Callum likes _____ cars, while his dad prefers older ones.

3. Spell:

He got a _____ compass for his maths set.

Spelling 4-12

4. Spell:

In ancient times _____ was made between goods because there was no money.

5. Spell:

Tom fell from his bike and cut his _____ lip.

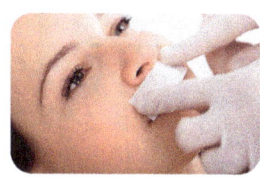

6. Spell:

Eating _____ helps grandpa to keep his blood pressure low.

Spelling 4-12

7. Spell:

Am _____ sure that it was Tony on that TV show lastnight!

8. Spell:

I wrote a five-page letter of _____ to the head of the school.

9. Spell:

Joseph was going to _____ Elliot as the deputy.

Spelling 4-12

10. Spell:

Please clean up your room when you

_____ studying.

11. Spell:

They had to line up in a _____ queue.

12. Spell:

_____ was a massive crowd at the concert.

Well done! You have finished lesson 12.

Spelling 4-13

1. Spell:

Have you, by any _____ , seen my glasses?

2. Spell:

I don't drink _____ with my friends at the bar.

3. Spell:

The twins were _____ of their brother's admission to the University to study medicine.

Spelling 4-13

4. Spell:

He was able to _____ the two boys who were fighting over a game.

5. Spell:

She pulled the _____ back to see the car parked in front of her house.

6. Spell:

The _____ had a chat with me after the long flight.

Spelling 4-13

7. Spell:

She felt a _____ pain in her abdomen.

8. Spell:

The chicken was _____ and well-cooked.

9. Spell:

Mondays are usually very _____ for me.

Spelling 4-13

10. Spell:

She had to watch her steps because the hallway was _____ .

11. Spell:

He wrote an _____ for the school magazine.

12. Spell:

The police did not _____ the boys after listening to their story.

You completed lesson 13! Bravo! You are doing a great job. Pretty soon, you will be an expert in spelling.

Spelling 4-14

1. Spell:

The _____ chopped the meat and packed them in the freezer.

2. Spell:

I _____ know the scores.

3. Spell:

Kelly bought her a fanciful _____ ring and necklace.

Spelling 4-14

4. Spell:

I _____ with all my heart for Tom's recovery from the accident.

5. Spell:

We travelled to _____ Island for the holidays.

6. Spell:

It is _____ to know that my drawing was the best in the competition.

Spelling 4-14

7. Spell:

The old lady was supported with a soft _____ .

8. Spell:

The little bird is _____ now in its nest.

9. Spell:

Every Sunday, mom visits grandma's _____ and leaves some flowers.

Spelling 4-14

10. Spell:

He took out his _____ and gave it to the wife to blow her nose.

11. Spell:

Scuba diving allows you to _____ the sea's depths.

12. Spell:

The pilot managed to fly the plane through the _____ .

Lesson 14 has come to an end. Awesome!

Spelling 4-15

1. Spell:
She was able to _____ her weekly spending, so she got a raise in her pocket money.

2. Spell:
She called her in the _____ and gave her the details.

3. Spell:
In ancient years, people used to write using ink and a _____ .

Spelling 4-15

4. Spell:

The seal was stuck to the _____, and a group of people helped her swim back to the sea.

5. Spell:

Dan lost his keys, so his dad gave him the _____ key.

6. Spell:

She had made a _____ to come early, but she broke her _____ .

Spelling 4-15

7. Spell:

She read the _____ and answered all the questions in her book.

8. Spell:

You can only go into the gym if you have a _____ card.

9. Spell:

The _____ is full of books.

Spelling 4-15

10. Spell:

She did _____ the room because of the visitors.

11. Spell:

The soldiers are _____ to their General.

12. Spell:

A thin _____ was seen in the dark when the robbery took place.

Look at you! You are natural! And it seems that you will be a spelling bee master pretty soon! You have just finished lesson 15.

Spelling 4-16

1. Spell:

For an _____ , I mistook his dog for my missing one.

2. Spell:

He will _____ a new family house on the plot of land.

3. Spell:

The _____ was not made clear at the start.

Spelling 4-16

4. Spell:

They sat around their grandma, listening to

_____ songs.

5. Spell:

There is always _____ , so we should be optimistic.

6. Spell:

The driver did slam on his _____ suddenly.

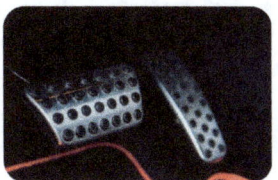

Spelling 4-16

7. Spell:

Your ornaments are _____! Did you make them yourself?

8. Spell:

_____ Rapunzel had long blonde hair with magical powers.

9. Spell:

_____ Everest is the tallest on earth.

Spelling 4-16

10. Spell:

Beatrice wears _____ hair.

11. Spell:

Her mummy _____ her when she heard her result and how much effort she put in.

12. Spell:

Musa likes to play _____ with Mohammed.

Look at you! You are natural! And it seems that you will be a spelling bee master pretty soon! You have just finished lesson 16.

Spelling 4-17

1. Spell:

She helped her mummy to _____ the hall for the occasion.

2. Spell:

I am looking forward to seeing the "Charlie and the Chocolate _____" movie on channel

3. Spell:

We have learned about _____ nouns in class.

Spelling 4-17

4. Spell:

There were _____ people involved in the incident.

5. Spell:

The pieces of the puzzle must be placed in _____ order.

6. Spell:

"Go out!" the driver _____ .

Spelling 4-17

7. Spell:

Are you _____ for what you have done to your sister?

8. Spell:

I had to do a _____ test to see if I was positive for Covid-19.

9. Spell:

After the thieves _____ their time in prison, they will be free.

Spelling 4-17

10. Spell:

Can you _____ more loudly, please?

11. Spell:

Let us not _____ at who should go first; we will all have a turn.

12. Spell:

The decision will _____ on my dad's view.

You completed lesson 17! Bravo! You are doing a great job.

Spelling 4-18

1. Spell:

_____ is everything.

2. Spell:

Hey, wait a _____ ! It's my turn!

3. Spell:

He read the book because it was of _____ to him.

Spelling 4-18

4. Spell:
Cinderella left the dance at _____ and lost her glass slipper on the steps as she left.

5. Spell:
She will _____ at home until she finds her purse.

6. Spell:
She does not _____ to have friends in her new school.

Spelling 4-18

7. Spell:

_____ my vacation this summer, I learned sea skiing.

8. Spell:
The announcement has been made _____ .

9. Spell:
The mother did _____ her baby while on her phone.

spelling 4-18

10. Spell:

Do you _____ you will score a goal?

11. Spell:

A _____ has four sides.

12. Spell:

I _____ if you can come to my house in the evening.

Lesson 18 has come to an end. Awesome! Keep up the excellent work! And

spelling 4-19

1. Spell:

The competition was _____ , and he still won.

2. Spell:

She did _____ the leftover food after everyone had had a second round.

3. Spell:

_____ can you help pick up the rubbish on the floor?

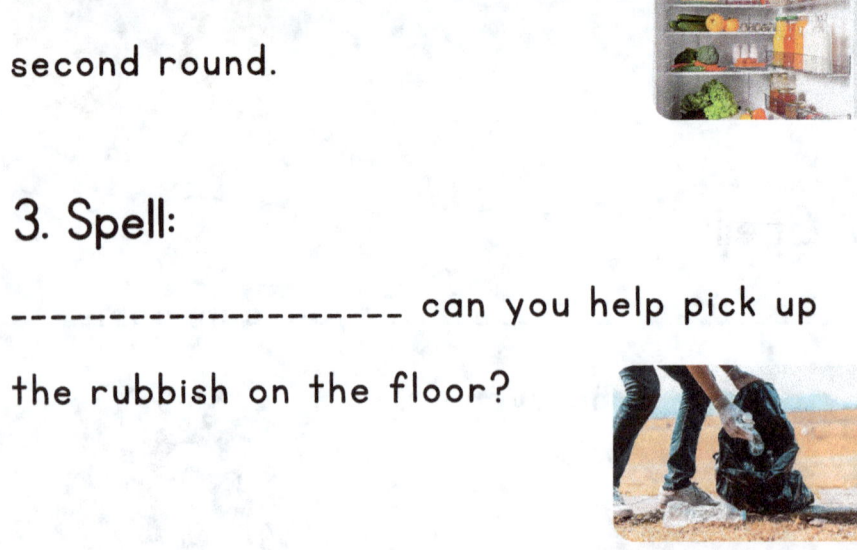

Spelling 4-19

4. Spell:

Nina came _____ in the class test.

5. Spell:

Gabriel came _____ in the class quiz.

6. Spell:

The carpenter has fixed the _____ door.

Spelling 4-19

7. Spell:
The dog is losing _____ , so we must immediately take him to the veterinarian.

8. Spell:
She was _____ in her narration.

9. Spell:
She was encouraged by the gentle and soothing _____ words spoken to her.

Spelling 4-19

10. Spell:

Grandma keeps and maintains a

_____ garden.

11. Spell:

There has been no _____ of

the plane since yesterday.

12. Spell:

_____ comes and goes, so I

prefer to stick to more

all-time classic clothes.

You have done excellent job finishing words in lesson 19.

Spelling 4-20

1. Spell:

The _____ of the factories ends up in the river.

2. Spell:

She went to _____ for the meaning of the word on the internet.

3. Spell:

He put his travel money in his trouser _____ .

Spelling 4-20

4. Spell:

Did you _____ that Jim lost his appetite today?

5. Spell:

He was able to translate the _____ into French and memorized it.

6. Spell:

Adam spent his pocket money to buy a small _____ for his mum.

Spelling 4-20

7. Spell:
He stood on the expansive balcony of his new hotel to have a nice _____ of the beach.

8. Spell:
Oliver is sitting _____ the tree.

9. Spell:
She laid her head on a soft _____ .

Spelling 4-20

10. Spell:

Can you _____ your reason for coming late?

11. Spell:

John is so funny, and I always _____ at his jokes!

12. Spell:

He used the _____ on his phone to take loads of pictures.

Congrats! You have made such Progress! You finished the words in lesson 20 already.

Spelling 4-21

1. Spell:

The _____ of the canteen food is reasonable.

2. Spell:

Her _____ did not come to pick her up on time, so she was sad.

3. Spell:

She made the school _____ on time.

Spelling 4-21

4. Spell:

_____ was Tuesday, and Today is Wednesday.

5. Spell:

Vivian had to _____ herself after the long hours of driving.

6. Spell:

Can I ask you a _____ , please?

Spelling 4-21

7. Spell:

The hungry lion gave a loud, scary

_____ at the zoo.

8. Spell:

Deborah is a very _____ girl

with good manners.

9. Spell:

I do not understand your point exactly;

could you give me an _____ ?

spelling 4-21

10. Spell:

Billy is well _____ of his timetable.

11. Spell:

Okay, now we have to control _____ to minimize our losses.

12. Spell:

You are making _____ progress in your spelling.

Wonderful! You have completed words in lesson 21. Keep up the excellent work, and don't forget: words matter, and most importantly, correctly written words matter.

Spelling 4-22

1. Spell:

The head boy gave a _____ speech at the assembly.

2. Spell:

The school bag could not _____ all the books, so I left the rest.

3. Spell:

The _____ is the difference between the highest and smallest numbers in a set of given data.

Spelling 4-22

4. Spell:
"Charlie and the Chocolate _____"
has been one of my favorite movies.

5. Spell:
Can you _____ the spelling of the word to my ear?

6. Spell:
Have you cast your _____ yet?

spelling 4-22

7. Spell:

Gold is the most precious _____ on earth.

8. Spell:

The _____ station is not too far from my house.

9. Spell:

I can feel the _____ of an insect on the leg.

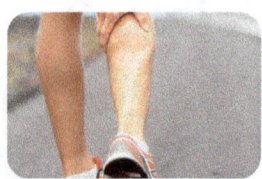

Spelling 4-22

10. Spell:

The lady is carrying a brown

_____ box.

11. Spell:

The carpenter came to _____

the floor length.

12. Spell:

Playing the _____ makes me

relax.

Lesson 22 has come to an end. Awesome! Keep up the excellent work!

Spelling 4-23

1. Spell:

He had a _____ success with his experiment.

2. Spell:

The teacher was not _____ the class's decision.

3. Spell:

Ding! It sounds like you have a new _____ in your inbox.

Spelling 4-23

4. Spell:

The red car stopped in the _____ of the road.

5. Spell:

It is very _____ that you write your name on your answer sheet.

6. Spell:

_____ is the finals, so I have to be at the stadium.

Spelling 4-23

7. Spell:
We are going to _____ house on Sunday to watch a film.

8. Spell:
You are well prepared for the exam, son, so there is no need to be _____ .

9. Spell:
James's bed has a _____ and a silver frame.

Spelling 4-23

10. Spell:

Metallica was a popular Heavy _____ band of the 80's.

11. Spell:

Nathan will _____ for a new job in January.

12. Spell:

The team did _____ high in the match.

Well done! You have finished lesson 23. You should be proud of yourself!

Spelling 4-24

1. Spell:

Lewis threw the apple core into the

_____ of the

garden.

2. Spell:

She did not _____ because

the lifeguard jumped in on time.

3. Spell:

Lucy did _____ attention in

class today.

Spelling 4-24

4. Spell:

The _____ starts at noon, so we must be there on time.

5. Spell:

The _____ starts at 7 pm, so we must get there early.

6. Spell:

Steven ignored the silly _____ his friends gave after walking down the stage.

Spelling 4-24

7. Spell:

Betty likes to play table _____ with her dad.

8. Spell:

The teacher corrected some _____ mistakes in my essay.

9. Spell:

I am _____ to see you are back from the hospital, Mary!

Spelling 4-24

10. Spell:
It's challenging to _____ a master's degree without studying hard.

11. Spell:
The _____ of the doll house was a real bargain!

12. Spell:
Nancy has a firm _____ in God.

You are so close to the end. Lesson 24 is complete. One more task is left, and you are done. Right? Okay, let's go!

spelling 4-25

1. Spell:

We all wish the war in Ukraine stops so the country can have _____ again.

2. Spell:

Mum? Have you _____ me the audio for my spelling course?

3. Spell:

He cut the card into halves with a pair of _____ .

Spelling 4-25

4. Spell:

He did not have enough _____ to walk up the stairs.

5. Spell:

I _____ the work of this painter because he uses such vivid colors!

6. Spell:

The nurse will _____ the new baby on a scale.

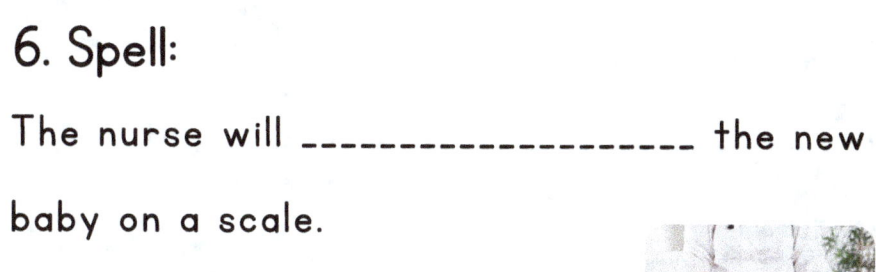

Spelling 4-25

7. Spell:

The train will leave the _____ at 4 pm.

8. Spell:

They make such a lovely _____! I hope their marriage is full of love and happiness.

9. Spell:

A _____ has four right angles.

Spelling 4-25

10. Spell:
The police caught the _____ running towards the main road.

11. Spell:
Kathrine planned a _____ visit to see her friend in a nearby village.

12. Spell:
A _____ has three sides.

Here we are! Last lesson, and you have reached the end of Spelling 4. Do you feel like you have conquered the vocabulary and spelling field?

Great! You should be proud of yourself. If, however, you do not feel very confident with some of the words, repeat them again and again until you fully understand the meaning of the orthography.

Conclusion

Congratulations! You little word champions!

You have finished one more book of the Spelling for Kids series: Spelling 4! Now give yourself a round of applause for getting this far.

It took time and effort for you to achieve it. But, you know what they say: success comes with hard work. And you are an example of it. I hope that finishing this book has made you feel more self-assured regarding not only your spelling skills but also your listening skills and your memory as well. And if you continue this course, you will see an upgrade in your confidence and knowledge.

There is no hurry, though. Everybody learns at a different pace and rhythm. But it is crucial to notice the spelling words that don't come easy to you and "nail them" by practicing more on them so you don't get to have any gaps in your studying. So, that's it, folks!

The next milestone is Spelling 5.

Are you ready?

Please leave a 1-click Review!

I would be incredibly thankful if you could take just 60 seconds to write a brief review on Amazon or the platform of purchase, even if it's just a few sentences!

Sneak Peek!

I would like to share with you a sneak peek into one of my other audiobooks that I think you would really enjoy. The audiobook is called "Spelling Five: An Interactive Vocabulary & Spelling Workbook for 9-Year-Olds. ," and it is a spelling book that covers words every teen must know and are frequently misspelled in exams. It is broken down into easy-to-follow spelling exercises that take only 10 minutes per day.

Hope you enjoy this free chapter!

Spelling 5-1

1. Spell:

Lydia had the rare _____ of speaking with the queen.

2. Spell:

Six and four make _____ ten.

3. Spell:

He will be there, _____ he may be a little bit late.

spelling 5-1

4. Spell:

They sat down at the beach to

_____ at the sea.

5. Spell:

She had _____ because of the pain she was having.

6. Spell:

The bus _____ did not give her a ticket because she was rude.

Spelling 5-1

7. Spell:
I pay _____ visits to my grandma because she is sick.

8. Spell:
She was able to _____ her teacher perfectly.

9. Spell:
She explained a different _____ which made more sense.

spelling 5-1

10. Spell:
The manager asked me to put a caution sign because the floor was _____ .

11. Spell:
Noah _____ figured out his dad's password.

12. Spell:
Oliver did not _____ the rude apology.

That's it for lesson 1. Well done!

Spelling 5-2

1. Spell:

Lisa chose to draw a _____

in today's drawing lesson.

2. Spell:

Nathan put his craft on the _____

table.

3. Spell:

He lost all his _____ in

gambling.

Spelling 5-2

4. Spell:

She did not have any _____ for tasty food because she was sick.

5. Spell:

In her maths book, Pricilla used _____ tracing paper to enlarge and rotate a shape.

6. Spell:

My family is _____ to me.

Spelling 5-2

7. Spell:
Lilian's dad and uncle tied the ship to the

_____ with firm

ropes.

8. Spell:
Everyone in the boy's scout admires

Emmanuel for his

_____ .

9. Spell:
My little sister has a great sense of

_____ which I also admire.

Spelling 5-2

10. Spell:

The _____ sang an uplifting and inspiring song at church on Sunday.

11. Spell:

Dylan bought a broken toy, so he returned it to _____ a refund.

12. Spell:

The cat did _____ Melissa's drawing.

Congrats! You have finished learning the words in lesson 2. Remember to know and understand the meaning of all the new words you have found.

spelling 5-3

1. Spell:

The dog was buried at the pet's

_____ last week.

2. Spell:

Will you be _____ to babysit

this weekend?

3. Spell:

The population of the city is, on

_____ , 100,000 people.

Spelling 5-3

4. Spell:

Yusuf was put in an _____ position with the question he picked.

5. Spell:

He got the cup at a lower price which is a real _____ .

6. Spell:

Lola had a _____ on her leg after the fall.

Spelling 5-3

7. Spell:

The items were sorted according to their different _____.

8. Spell:

The _____ have twelve members who are not active.

9. Spell:

She was able to _____ verbally and in writing to impress the teacher.

spelling 5-3

10. Spell:
I live in a small _____ with farmers.

11. Spell:
The _____ is coming up in January.

12. Spell:
Cecelia went to apologize because she had a guilty _____ .

Great! You have finished learning the words in lesson 3.

Spelling 5-4

1. Spell:

Amy had to hold her baby brother carefully because he was still _____ after his operations.

2. Spell:

The first-floor _____ is too low.

3. Spell:

Be careful with that glass because it is _____ .

Spelling 5-4

4. Spell:
The caretaker has failed to _____ his daily obligations.

5. Spell:
Nathan dares not to _____ in Sofia's personal life.

6. Spell:
Julius lost a lot of money in a failed business _____ that he embarked on with his friend.

Spelling 5-4

7. Spell:

Lydia's mum was sick, so she got a close _____ to look after her.

8. Spell:

Kenneth will _____ tomorrow if it is warm enough to go and swim.

9. Spell:

Jude came _____ in the skipping competition.

spelling 5-4

10. Spell:

In the summer, Jude and James mow their

_____ once a

week.

11. Spell:

The school's playing field has an

_____ shape that is decent.

12. Spell:

The tower block has a _____

foundation.

Great! Lesson 4 is over! I suggest you get some rest before going on to the next lesson. That will help you recharge and return to the next task more refreshed! Great work!

Spelling 5-5

1. Spell:

The famous singer used _____ with her makeup to look more glowing on stage.

2. Spell:

We grow and _____ our vegetables in our garden.

3. Spell:

Evie did not _____ her doctor's appointment, so she got a message from the hospital.

Spelling 5-5

4. Spell:

You must grab him and _____

him to go through the back

door.

5. Spell:

Tyler's _____ was wrong,

but Tony's was right.

6. Spell:

The police arrived on time at the crime

_____ ,which saved Eddy.

Spelling 5-5

7. Spell:

Andrei and Molly made a footprint in the wet _____ .

8. Spell:

A _____ is made up of hundred years.

9. Spell:

Chloe did not _____ her sister to tidy up her room because she was running late.

Spelling 5-5

10. Spell:

The _____ decided on the case and gave his judgment.

11. Spell:

Faisal's _____ salary has been increased because of his hard work and good contributions.

12. Spell:

When I go abroad, I always buy goods from _____ stores.

Fantastic! You have finished the words in lesson 5. What a task!

Answers

Spelling 4-1

1. Spell: Mountain
2. Spell: Heavy
3. Spell: Breakfast
4. Spell: Straight
5. Spell: Shoulder
6. Spell: Apart
7. Spell: Shape
8. Spell: Pair
9. Spell: Screw
10. Spell: Alive
11. Spell: Power
12. Spell: Law

Spelling 4-2

1. Spell: Valley
2. Spell: Journey
3. Spell: Season
4. Spell: Regions
5. Spell: Sandwich
6. Spell: Excellent
7. Spell: Tough
8. Spell: Begin
9. Spell: Distant
10. Spell: Suppose
11. Spell: Passenger
12. Spell: Follow

Answers

Spelling 4-3

1. Spell: <u>Chapter</u>
2. Spell: <u>Flight</u>
3. Spell: <u>Product</u>
4. Spell: <u>Written</u>
5. Spell: <u>Tore</u>
6. Spell: <u>Soil</u>
7. Spell: <u>View</u>
8. Spell: <u>Birth</u>
9. Spell: <u>Poem</u>
10. Spell: <u>Whip</u>
11. Spell: <u>Quite</u>
12. Spell: <u>Price</u>

Spelling 4-4

1. Spell: <u>Conduct</u>
2. Spell: <u>Startle</u>
3. Spell: <u>Refused</u>
4. Spell: <u>Expensive</u>
5. Spell: <u>Chimney</u>
6. Spell: <u>Pour</u>
7. Spell: <u>Writing</u>
8. Spell: <u>Course</u>
9. Spell: <u>Anger</u>
10. Spell: <u>Obey</u>
11. Spell: <u>Coin</u>
12. Spell: <u>Idea</u>

Answers

Spelling 4-5

1. Spell: Grandfather
2. Spell: Relative
3. Spell: Pleasure
4. Spell: Torch
5. Spell: Chocolate
6. Spell: Avenue
7. Spell: Dawn
8. Spell: Wage
9. Spell: Term
10. Spell: Fellow
11. Spell: Double
12. Spell: Depart

Spelling 4-6

1. Spell: Weary
2. Spell: Autumn
3. Spell: Current
4. Spell: Parcel
5. Spell: Employ
6. Spell: Obey
7. Spell: Weather
8. Spell: Equal
9. Spell: Death
10. Spell: Spoil
11. Spell: Crowd
12. Spell: Difficult

Answers

Spelling 4-7

1. Spell: <u>Compel</u>
2. Spell: <u>Occur</u>
3. Spell: <u>Vegetables</u>
4. Spell: <u>Excite</u>
5. Spell: <u>Giant</u>
6. Spell: <u>Vessel</u>
7. Spell: <u>Insect</u>
8. Spell: <u>Towel</u>
9. Spell: <u>Avoid</u>
10. Spell: <u>Newspaper</u>
11. Spell: <u>Bicycle</u>
12. Spell: <u>However</u>

Spelling 4-8

1. Spell: <u>Awful</u>
2. Spell: <u>Prefix</u>
3. Spell: <u>Success</u>
4. Spell: <u>Person</u>
5. Spell: <u>Try</u>
6. Spell: <u>Possible</u>
7. Spell: <u>Select</u>
8. Spell: <u>Vote</u>
9. Spell: <u>Active</u>
10. Spell: <u>Sorry</u>
11. Spell: <u>Gentle</u>
12. Spell: <u>Daughter</u>

Answers

Spelling 4-9

1. Spell: Coffee
2. Spell: Length
3. Spell: Enemy
4. Spell: Reply
5. Spell: Heart
6. Spell: Uniform
7. Spell: Discuss
8. Spell: Circle
9. Spell: Citizen
10. Spell: Piece
11. Spell: Cheap
12. Spell: Kettle

Spelling 4-10

1. Spell: Kettle
2. Spell: Honest
3. Spell: Tour
4. Spell: Hurry
5. Spell: Steady
6. Spell: Address
7. Spell: Account
8. Spell: Value
9. Spell: Picnic
10. Spell: Travel
11. Spell: Color (US) Colourful (UK)
12. Spell: Join

Answers

Spelling 4-11

1. Spell: Electric
2. Spell: Deliver
3. Spell: Control
4. Spell: Shelter
5. Spell: Journey
6. Spell: Display
7. Spell: Between
8. Spell: Wrote
9. Spell: Village
10. Spell: Courage
11. Spell: Escape
12. Spell: Favor (US) Favour (UK)

Spelling 4-12

1. Spell: Ought
2. Spell: Modern
3. Spell: Spare
4. Spell: Trade
5. Spell: Upper
6. Spell: Healthy
7. Spell: Pretty
8. Spell: Complaint
9. Spell: Appoint
10. Spell: Finish
11. Spell: Single
12. Spell: There

Answers

Spelling 4-13

1. Spell: Chance
2. Spell: Beer
3. Spell: Proud
4. Spell: Calm
5. Spell: Curtain
6. Spell: Captain
7. Spell: Sudden
8. Spell: Tender
9. Spell: Busy
10. Spell: Slippery
11. Spell: Article
12. Spell: Arrest

Spelling 4-14

1. Spell: Butcher
2. Spell: Already
3. Spell: Diamond
4. Spell: Prayed
5. Spell: Adventure
6. Spell: Wonderful
7. Spell: Cushion
8. Spell: Safe
9. Spell: Grave
10. Spell: Handkerchief
11. Spell: Explore
12. Spell: Lightning

Answers

Spelling 4-15

1. Spell: Manage
2. Spell: Evening
3. Spell: Feather
4. Spell: Shore
5. Spell: Master
6. Spell: Promise
7. Spell: Passage
8. Spell: Member
9. Spell: Shelf
10. Spell: Decorate
11. Spell: Obedient
12. Spell: Figure

Spelling 4-16

1. Spell: Instant
2. Spell: Build
3. Spell: Point
4. Spell: Folk
5. Spell: Tomorrow
6. Spell: Brake
7. Spell: Lovely
8. Spell: Princess
9. Spell: Mountain
10. Spell: Natural
11. Spell: Surprised
12. Spell: Cricket

Answers

Spelling 4-17

1. Spell: Decorate
2. Spell: Factory
3. Spell: Proper
4. Spell: Several
5. Spell: Perfect
6. Spell: Exclaims
7. Spell: Sorry
8. Spell: Rapid
9. Spell: Serve
10. Spell: Speak
11. Spell: Whinge
12. Spell: Hinge

Spelling 4-18

1. Spell: Family
2. Spell: Minute
3. Spell: Interest
4. Spell: Midnight
5. Spell: Remain
6. Spell: Appear
7. Spell: During
8. Spell: Public
9. Spell: Abandon
10. Spell: Reckon
11. Spell: Square
12. Spell: Wonder

Answers

Spelling 4-19

1. Spell: <u>Fierce</u>
2. Spell: <u>Freeze</u>
3. Spell: <u>Please</u>
4. Spell: <u>Second</u>
5. Spell: <u>Fourth</u>
6. Spell: <u>Entrance</u>
7. Spell: <u>Blood</u>
8. Spell: <u>Sincere</u>
9. Spell: <u>Positive</u>
10. Spell: <u>Beautiful</u>
11. Spell: <u>Sign</u>
12. Spell: <u>Fashion</u>

Spelling 4-20

1. Spell: <u>Waste</u>
2. Spell: <u>Search</u>
3. Spell: <u>Pocket</u>
4. Spell: <u>Notice</u>
5. Spell: <u>Verse</u>
6. Spell: <u>Jewel</u>
7. Spell: <u>View</u>
8. Spell: <u>Beneath</u>
9. Spell: <u>Cushion</u>
10. Spell: <u>Explain</u>
11. Spell: <u>Laugh</u>
12. Spell: <u>Camera</u>

Answers

Spelling 4-21

1. Spell: Price
2. Spell: Parent
3. Spell: Payment
4. Spell: Yesterday
5. Spell: Stretch
6. Spell: Question
7. Spell: Roar
8. Spell: Polite
9. Spell: Example
10. Spell: Ahead
11. Spell: Damage
12. Spell: Steady

Spelling 4-22

1. Spell: Powerful
2. Spell: Contain
3. Spell: Range
4. Spell: Factory
5. Spell: Whisper
6. Spell: Vote
7. Spell: Metal
8. Spell: Railway
9. Spell: Movement
10. Spell: Leather
11. Spell: Measure
12. Spell: Piano

Answers

Spelling 4-23

1. Spell: Huge
2. Spell: Against
3. Spell: Message
4. Spell: Middle
5. Spell: Important
6. Spell: Tonight
7. Spell: Their
8. Spell: Anxious
9. Spell: Copper
10. Spell: Metal
11. Spell: Apply
12. Spell: Score

Spelling 4-24

1. Spell: Center (US) Centre (UK)
2. Spell: Drown
3. Spell: Attract
4. Spell: Program (US) Programme (UK)
5. Spell: Concert
6. Spell: Remark
7. Spell: Tennis
8. Spell: Minor
9. Spell: Happy
10. Spell: Obtain
11. Spell: Purchase
12. Spell: Belief

Answers

Spelling 4-25

1. Spell: Peace
2. Spell: Bought
3. Spell: Scissors
4. Spell: Strength
5. Spell: Admire
6. Spell: Weigh
7. Spell: Station
8. Spell: Couple
9. Spell: Square
10. Spell: Thief
11. Spell: Surprise
12. Spell: Triangle

Spelling 5-1

1. Spell: Opportunity
2. Spell: Altogether
3. Spell: Although
4. Spell: Marvel
5. Spell: Groaned
6. Spell: Conductor
7. Spell: Frequent
8. Spell: Describe
9. Spell: Angle
10. Spell: Slippery
11. Spell: Easily
12. Spell: Accept

Answers

Spelling 5-2

1. Spell: Donkey
2. Spell: Display
3. Spell: Wealth
4. Spell: Appetite
5. Spell: Transparent
6. Spell: Precious
7. Spell: Quay
8. Spell: Bravery
9. Spell: Style
10. Spell: Choir
11. Spell: Demand
12. Spell: Destroy

Spelling 5-3

1. Spell: Cemetery
2. Spell: Available
3. Spell: Average
4. Spell: Awkward
5. Spell: Bargain
6. Spell: Bruise
7. Spell: Category
8. Spell: Committee
9. Spell: Communicate
10. Spell: Community
11. Spell: Competition
12. Spell: Conscience

Answers

Spelling 5-4

1. Spell: Delicate
2. Spell: Ceiling
3. Spell: Fragile
4. Spell: Fulfill (US)
   Fulfil (UK)
5. Spell: Meddle
6. Spell: Venture
7. Spell: Relative
8. Spell: Decide
9. Spell: Ninth
10. Spell: Lawn
11. Spell: Oval
12. Spell: Solid

Spelling 5-5

1. Spell: Glitter
2. Spell: Collect
3. Spell: Cancel
4. Spell: Propel
5. Spell: Guess
6. Spell: Scene
7. Spell: Cement
8. Spell: Century
9. Spell: Compel
10. Spell: Judge
11. Spell: Annual
12. Spell: Local

Other Books You'll Love!

1. **Spelling one: An Interactive Vocabulary & Spelling** Workbook for 5-Year-Olds. (With Audiobook Lessons)

2. **Spelling Two: An Interactive Vocabulary & Spelling** Workbook for 6-Year-Olds. (With Audiobook Lessons)

3. **Spelling Three: An Interactive Vocabulary & Spelling** Workbook for 7-Year-Olds. (With Audiobook Lessons)

4. **Spelling Four: An Interactive Vocabulary & Spelling** Workbook for 8-Year-Olds. (With Audiobook Lessons)

5. **Spelling Five: An Interactive Vocabulary & Spelling** Workbook for 9-Year-Olds. (With Audiobook Lessons)

6. **Spelling Six: An Interactive Vocabulary & Spelling** Workbook for 10 & 11 Years Old. (With Audiobook Lessons)

7. **Spelling Seven: An Interactive Vocabulary & Spelling** Workbook for 12-14 Years-Old. (With Audiobook Lessons)

Other Books You'll Love!

8. Raising Boys in Today's Digital World:
Proven Positive Parenting Tips for Raising Respectful, Successful, and Confident Boys

9. Raising Girls in Today's Digital World:
Proven Positive Parenting Tips for Raising Respectful, Successful, and Confident Girls

10. Raising Kids in Today's Digital World:
Proven Positive Parenting Tips for Raising Respectful, Successful, and Confident Kids

11. The Child Development and Positive Parenting Master Class 2-in-1 Bundle:
Proven Methods for Raising Well-Behaved and Intelligent Children, with Accelerated Learning Methods

12. Parenting Teens in Today's Challenging World 2-in-1 Bundle: Proven Methods for Improving Teenager's Behaviour with Positive Parenting and Family Communication

13. Life Strategies for Teenagers:
Positive Parenting, Tips and Understanding Teens for Better Communication and a Happy Family

14. Parenting Teen Girls in Today's Challenging World:
Proven Methods for Improving Teenager's Behaviour with Whole Brain Training

Other Books You'll Love!

15. Parenting Teen Boys in Today's Challenging World:
Proven Methods for Improving Teenager's Behaviour with Whole Brain Training

16. 101 Tips For Helping With Your Child's Learning:
Proven Strategies for Accelerated Learning and Raising Smart Children Using Positive Parenting Skills

17. 101 Tips for Child Development:
Proven Methods for Raising Children and Improving Kids Behavior with Whole Brain Training

18. Financial Tips to Help Kids:
Proven Methods for Teaching Kids Money Management and Financial Responsibility

19. Healthy Habits for Kids:
Positive Parenting Tips for Fun Kids Exercises, Healthy Snacks, and Improved Kids Nutrition

20. Mini Habits for Happy Kids:
Proven Parenting Tips for Positive Discipline and Improving Kids' Behavior

21. Good Habits for Healthy Kids 2-in-1 Combo Pack:
Proven Positive Parenting Tips for Improving Kid's Fitness and Children's Behavior

22. Raising Teenagers to Choose Wisely:
Keeping your Teen Secure in a Big World

23. Tips for #CollegeLife:
Powerful College Advice for Excelling as a College Freshman

Other Books You'll Love!

24. **The Career Success Formula:**
Proven Career Development Advice and Finding Rewarding Employment for Young Adults and College Graduates

25. **The Motivated Young Adult's Guide to Career Success and Adulthood:**
Proven Tips for Becoming a Mature Adult, Starting a Rewarding Career, and Finding Life Balance

26. **Bedtime Stories for Kids:**
Short Funny Stories and poems Collection for Children and Toddlers

27. **Guide for Boarding School Life**

28. **The Fear of The Lord:**
How God's Honour Guarantees Your Peace

Audiobooks

Are available at any of the following retailers:

1. Kobo
https://www.kobo.com/us/en/audiobook/spelling-four

2. Google Store
https://play.google.com/store/audiobooks/details/Bukky_Ekine_Ogunl ana_Spelling_Four?id=AQAAAEAi-yC7EM

3. Libro
https://libro.fm/audiobooks/9798368926681

4. Storytel
https://www.storytel.com/se/sv/books/4262065

5. Scribd
https://www.scribd.com/audiobook/637100019/Spelling-Four-An-Interactive-Vocabulary-and-Spelling-Workbook-for-8-Year-Olds-With-AudioBook-Lessons

6. Barnes and Noble
https://www.barnesandnoble.com/w/spelling-four-bukky-ekine-ogunlana/1143328243

7. Spotify
https://open.spotify.com/show/0i6ZYRi68kk2bXmp8NYMbQ

8. Hoopladigital

https://www.hoopladigital.com/title/15980153

9. Chirpbooks
https://www.chirpbooks.com/audiobooks/spelling-four-by-bukky-ekine-ogunlana

And all other audiobook retailers!

Facebook Community

I invite you to our Facebook community group to visit this link and simply click the join group.

https://www.facebook.com/groups/397683731371863

This is a private group where parents, teachers, and carers can learn, share tips, ask questions, and discuss and get valuable content about raising and parenting modern children.

It is a very supportive and encouraging group where valuable content, free resources, and exciting discussion about parenting are shared. You can use this to benefit from social media.

You will learn a lot from schoolteachers, experts, counselors, and new and experienced parents, and stay updated with our latest releases.

See you there!

And all other audiobook retailers!

Your Free Gift

Your Free Gift!

As a way of saying thank you for Your purchase, I have included a gift that you can download at

TCEC publishing .com

References

[1] https://www.theseus.fi/bitstream/handle/10024/50239/Anttila_Marianna_Saikkonen_Pinja.pdf

[2] https://www.researchgate.net/publication/283721084_Early_Reading_Development

[3] https://www2.ed.gov/parents/academic/help/adolescence/adolescence.pdf

[4] http://centerforchildwelfare.org/kb/prprouthome/Helping%20Your%20Children%20Navigate%20Their%20Teenage%20Years.pdf

[5] https://www.childrensmn.org/images/family_resource_pdf/027121.pdf

[6] https://educationnorthwest.org/sites/default/files/develop-ing-empathy-in-children--and-youth.pdf

[7] https://www.researchgate.net/publication/263227023_Family_Time_Activities_and_Adolescents'_Emotional_Well-be-ing_

[8] http://www.delmarlearning.com/companions/content/1418019224/AdditionalSupport/box11.1.pdf

[9] https://exeter.anglican.org/wp-content/uploads/2014/11/Lis-tening-to-children-leaflet_NCB.pdf

[10] https://www.researchgate.net/publication/312600262_Creative_Thinking_among_Preschool_Children

www.ingramcontent.com/pod-product-compliance
Lightning Source LLC
Chambersburg PA
CBHW050241120526
44590CB00016B/2182